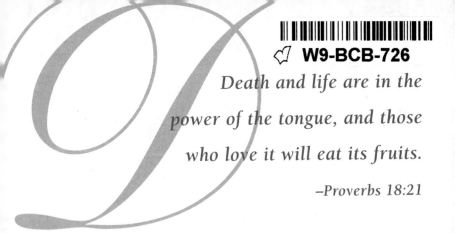

Death and life are in the power of the tongue, and those who love it will eat its fruits.

–Proverbs 18:21

The Power *of* Words

Nancy Leigh DeMoss

CONTENTS

A Word from Nancy

Dear friend,

During the next four weeks, we're going to consider what may be the most powerful member of our body— the tongue! Did you know that there are more than 100 references to the tongue in the book of Proverbs alone?

Proverbs 18:21 puts it this way: *"Death and life are in the power of the tongue, and those who love it will eat its fruits."* Think about it! Our words can give life . . . or they can give death. One way or the other, the words we speak have results.

It's easy to feel discouraged when we think about the words that come out of our mouths, but the purpose of this devotional study is to give hope! Together, let's look to Jesus Christ, the Living Word, who brings healing and life. As we look into His Word, may He transform us into His likeness, by the power of His Holy Spirit.

A fellow traveler,

Nancy

Nancy Leigh DeMoss

Week One

THE POWER AND IMPACT OF WORDS

Memory Verse

*"Death and life are in the power of the tongue,
and those who love it will eat its fruits."*
Proverbs 18:21

(Use the lines below to jot down any insights that the Lord gives you into this verse or any specific ways that it applies to your life this week.)

_____

_____

_____

_____

All too often, we throw out words without thinking of the consequences. This week we're going to look at the power and impact of our words. I'd encourage you to memorize Proverbs 18:21; meditate on it throughout the week, and ask the Lord to bring these words to life.

Our words can do enormous good—or enormous damage. They can be life-giving—or life destroying. Proverbs 10:11 reminds us that our words can be like a spring of refreshing water to a weary traveler. My friend, God is our fountain. He alone can motivate and enable us to speak words that give true life.

Day One

A DEVASTATING FIRE

*"So also the tongue is a small member, yet it boasts
of great things. How great a forest is set ablaze by such a
small fire! And the tongue is a fire . . . ."*
James 3:5–6

On August 24, 2000, a 46-year-old woman tossed a burning match onto the ground when she stopped by the road to light a cigarette. Rather than putting out the burning match, she just glanced at it and left the area.[1] Many days later, the fire she had recklessly begun was finally contained. Timber worth more than 40 million dollars was destroyed, and over 80,000 acres were burned.

It's easy to hear this story and think, *How dare she leave a burning match in a dry forest?* Yet how often do we throw out our words without thinking about the consequences? We may even walk away after saying words that deeply wound others—not wanting to look at the enormous damage that we have caused.

Too often I talk without thinking, never considering the one receiving my words. It's easy to blurt out words when we're under pressure. Although we may have no intention of hurting others, our words can inflict great damage. Much like a burned forest, the damage can take years to restore.

Recall a time when the words you said resulted in consequences you didn't intend. Describe what happened:

_____

_____

_____

_____

"A gentle tongue is a tree of life, but perverseness in it breaks the spirit" (Proverbs 15:4). What does this verse say to you?

_____

_____

_____

_____

"Gracious words are like a honeycomb, sweetness to the soul and health to the body" (Proverbs 16:24). Describe a time when someone said especially encouraging words to you, and explain how God used those words to bless you.

_____

_____

_____

_____

How can you encourage someone with your words today?

_____

_____

_____

_____

Day Two

LIVING WITH CONSEQUENCES

"A gentle tongue is a tree of life,
but perverseness in it breaks the spirit."
Proverbs 15:4

Our words can do enormous damage. Even one thoughtless word has consequences. Proverbs 15:4 reminds us that wholesome words give life. It's hard to believe that the same tongue that speaks those life-giving words can also speak words that bring destruction.

Perhaps you heard such destructive words as a child . . . words you've never been able to forget. Even though you know today that those words weren't true, they still hurt deeply. You can still hear them ring in your heart: *You're dumb. You won't amount to anything. I wish you'd never been born.*

We can't control the words that are spoken to us. But we can focus on the words that we say to others. Sometimes it's easy for me to say careless or destructive words without thinking when I'm with those I know the best. It's when I'm with my family, a close friend, or a dear colleague that I often let down my guard and say discouraging, impatient words—words that wound rather than heal.

Many times we are blinded concerning how our words offend. We need to ask the Lord to open our eyes to ways that our words are hurtful or damaging. May our words give grace, blessing, and hope to those around us.

Think about the words you've spoken in the past 24 hours —at home, work, church, on the phone, etc. Were your words life-giving or destructive? Give an example of each:

_____

_____

_____

_____

"The wise lay up knowledge, but the mouth of a fool brings ruin near" (Proverbs 10:14). Ask the Lord to show you any adjustments you need to make in what you say or in how you say it. Describe what He has put on your heart:

_____

_____

_____

_____

Do you ever blurt out words that you wish you hadn't said? What can you do to remind yourself to think before you speak?

_____

_____

_____

Who do you know who weighs his/her words carefully before speaking? How does this affect the person's communication?

_____

_____

_____

Day Three

THE POWER TO HEAL

*"Gracious words are like a honeycomb,
sweetness to the soul and health to the body."*
Proverbs 16:24

Sit back, my friend, and close your eyes. Recall a time when someone said words that really encouraged you. Perhaps it was your mom or dad who said, "I believe in you!" Or maybe a good friend uttered those needed words of affirmation, "Don't give up! You can do it." Or, possibly a teacher's words were all you needed when she said, "You have a real gift in this area!"

I can't see you, but you probably have a smile on your face! Scripture tells us, "Gracious words are like a honeycomb, sweetness to the soul and health to the body." Notice the relationship between the body and soul—we can't separate the two. Sweet words can minister spiritual and physical blessing and health.

Honey is a natural sweetener that boosts energy. Likewise, words of encouragement boost our spirits. I'm so grateful for people who speak affirming words into my life. I thank God for the healing words of my family and friends. But I don't want to just be the beneficiary of encouragement. I want to be an encourager to others.

May we speak healing words that promote good health—words filled with grace, blessing, and hope.

What are some words that have really encouraged you and why?

_____

_____

_____

_____

Why do you think encouraging words promote good health?

_____

_____

_____

_____

_____

"By the blessing of the upright a city is exalted" (Proverbs 11:11a). Godly words can actually bring good to an entire community. Can you think of an example of how someone's encouraging words affected a whole community?

_____

_____

_____

_____

Think of someone who needs encouragement today. Jot down a plan for sharing healing words with this person, and then follow your plan.

_____

_____

_____

_____

Day Four

SUPERIOR QUALITY

"The tongue of the righteous is choice silver."
Proverbs 10:20

As we learned earlier, there are more than 100 references to the tongue in the book of Proverbs. In that book alone, I counted twelve verses where the word "heart" is mentioned in connection with the tongue.

Godly people speak out of the overflow of a godly heart. They are spiritually minded and don't just speak about spiritual things on Sundays. They are restrained and think before they speak. Proverbs describes the tongue of the righteous as choice silver.

So, *how do people get tongues of righteousness?* Well, their hearts are connected to the Source of wisdom and grace—the One who reveals Himself in Scripture.

I want to be a wise, godly woman, but I don't always want to pay the price for a heart of wisdom. It takes discipline and effort to fill our hearts with God's Word—and to have a tongue that is choice silver.

"Choice silver"—think about these two words. Silver, of course, is a prized metal. The tongue of the righteous is excellent, superior, worthy—it is *choice* silver—it has been carefully refined and is of the highest possible quality.

A heart that is rooted in the Word and character of God will bring forth words that are superior quality. Those words will be of great value to those who hear them.

It has been said that the words we speak are a thermometer of our hearts—they register the temperature (or condition) of our hearts. Why is this true?

_____

_____

_____

_____

 Based on the way you talk to others, what is the temperature of your heart?

_____

_____

_____

_____

 What words have one or both of your parents said that enriched your life? If you're a parent, what words can you speak to your children today that will be "choice silver"?

_____

_____

_____

_____

 What are some specific ways your words can bless and enrich the lives of those around you today? What practical things can you do to draw upon the Source of wisdom and grace?

_____

_____

_____

_____

Day Five

A GOOD REPORT

*"I do not cease to give thanks for you,
remembering you in my prayers."
Ephesians 1:16*

Although it happened more than two decades ago, it seems like yesterday. I had been unjustly slandered; my reputation and my pride had been hurt. Although I was devastated at the time, I can look back and see how God used that incident to mature me in several areas. One valuable lesson I learned was the damage we do when we spread an "evil report" about another person.

There have been times when I have put another servant of the Lord in a bad light by repeating needless information. As a result, I have had to make calls and write letters asking for forgiveness. Having to humble myself and deal with those issues has caused me to be more careful about what I say about others!

If we approach God in humility, He will convict us when our words do not please Him. Ask, "Is this a good report of this person? Have I verified the facts? Are my words kind and necessary?"

Here's a good test for both our thoughts and our words: "Finally, brothers, whatever is true, whatever is honorable, whatever is just, whatever is pure, whatever is lovely, whatever is commendable, if there is any excellence, if there is anything worthy of praise, think about these things" (Philippians 4:8).

Someone has said that flattery is saying things to others that I would not say behind their backs, and slander is saying things behind someone's back that I would not say in front of the person. Why does God hate flattery and slander?

_____

_____

_____

_____

Explain Jesus' words in Matthew 7:5, *"You hypocrite, first take the log out of your own eye, and then you will see clearly to take the speck out of your brother's eye."*

_____

_____

_____

_____

A faithful witness gives an accurate and truthful report. Can you recall a time that you were not a faithful witness?

_____

_____

_____

_____

Have your words this week been true, honorable, just, pure, lovely, commendable? Are you inclined to focus on the excellent things and those things worthy of praise, or do you tend to focus on negative things you can complain about?

_____

_____

_____

Prayer

Merciful Lord, reveal to me how my words are hurtful and damaging. Show me how to speak words that give grace, blessing, and hope.

I confess that often I want to justify and trivialize the things I say when they really reflect a heart issue. Give me a repentant heart. Fill my heart in such a way that its overflow will be the fruit of the Holy Spirit. Change my heart—and may my words bring glory and honor to You.

Amen.

Week Two

WORDS: A MIRROR OF THE HEART

Memory Verse

*"I have stored up your word in my heart,
that I might not sin against you."*
Psalm 119:11

(Record insights from this verse or ways that you apply it in your life this week.)

_____

_____

_____

_____

I hope you are being challenged by our brief study on the tongue, and that God is giving you a greater motivation to speak encouraging, life-giving words.

Perhaps you, like me, want to change some of your words. The key to a transformed tongue is a transformed heart. A person who is righteous loves what God loves and hates what He hates.

Jesus said, "The good person out of the good treasure of his heart produces good . . . for out of the abundance of the heart his mouth speaks" (Luke 6:45). This week we'll learn how the words we speak actually reflect our hearts.

If I am a foolish person, then I will speak foolish words. If I am a wicked person, I will speak wicked words. But if I am a godly woman whose heart is connected to Jesus Christ, then I will speak wise words that are full of grace, mercy, and truth.

Day One

HEART CONDITIONS

*"The heart of the wise man makes his speech judicious
and adds persuasiveness to his lips."*
Proverbs 16:23

Do you sometimes trivialize your words by saying things like "I didn't mean that. It just came out"? Unfortunately, the truth is that we really do mean what we say—our words reveal what's really in our heart.

I think about careless or hurtful words I have said to family members, co-workers, and friends—words I regret and wish I could take back. But we can't take back our words.

According to God's Word, all of us sin with our tongues (James 3:2); we need to confess our sin and turn from it. We need to take responsibility for our words, agree with God about what our words reveal about our hearts, and ask the Lord to change our hearts so we can speak words that heal.

Today, may we allow God to transform our hearts by the power of His Holy Spirit. When our hearts are filled with Him and with His wisdom and grace, we will speak wise, gracious words that bless and instruct others.

What is an instance in which you trivialized your words?

_____

_____

_____

_____

 Ask the Lord to reveal to you words you've spoken that dishonored Him. Write a brief prayer below expressing repentance for those words and for the heart condition they revealed.

_____

_____

_____

_____

 How can a wise man's words "add persuasiveness" in those who hear?

_____

_____

_____

_____

 Jot down a time when someone spoke wise words of instruction to you. How did these words affect your life?

_____

_____

_____

_____

Day Two

PERFECT NOONDAY

"For I am the Lord, I change not."
Malachi 3:6a (KJV)

We live in a world that is constantly changing. Innovative technology, updated styles, news at a moment's notice—sometimes it seems that nothing stays the same.

Yet Scripture tells us that the Lord never changes! He is "the same yesterday and today and forever" (Hebrews 13:8). The Lord is not like shifting sand. He is perfect noonday. There is no shadow of truth with our Lord. He does not flip-flop on issues, depending on His audience. He is always true.

I cannot say that my words have always been true. As a young woman in my twenties, wanting to make a good impression on others, I would sometimes exaggerate the truth. God showed me that my pride had resulted in a root of deception in my heart. By His grace, God granted me repentance. Over a period of time, He removed those roots of deceit and replaced them with truthfulness.

Spiritual victories are won when we speak the truth. In real life, it often seems that people who lie succeed. But Proverbs says that in the long run, the effect of true words will be enduring and those who deceive will not last.

🍇 *"The righteous hate falsehood"* (Proverbs 13:5). Explain how your own life demonstrates your hatred or tolerance of falsehood.

_____

_____

_____

_____

🍇 Second Corinthians 8:21 (NIV) says, *"For we are taking pains to do what is right . . . in the eyes of men."* Share a time when you knowingly left a false impression, even though your words were true.

_____

_____

_____

_____

🍇 Exaggeration overstates or embellishes details to make something more interesting. Do you sometimes exaggerate your accomplishments. If so, why?

_____

_____

_____

🍇 *"Lying lips are an abomination to the LORD, but those who act faithfully are his delight"* (Proverbs 12:22a). Share an example of a time when you (or someone you know) told the truth—even though the truth hurt.

_____

_____

_____

Day Three

TO TELL THE TRUTH

"Pray for us: for we trust we have a good conscience,
in all things willing to live honestly."
Hebrews 13:18 (KJV)

This particular church service was some twenty years ago, but I can still remember how miserable I was sitting in that pew, under the heavy hand of the Spirit's conviction. You see, a few years earlier, as a college student, I had lied on a number of weekly reports we had to turn in to our department. I knew I had to go back to my professor and make it right.

Because of my desire to be completely truthful in my communication, when I was a young woman the Lord led me to make the following commitment: *to speak the truth to every person, in every situation, regardless of the cost.* I have also committed that *anytime I fail to speak the truth, I will go back and make it right.* I've had to confess being untruthful, both privately and publicly; as a result, I've experienced the great freedom and joy of having a clear conscience before God and others.

As we get the truth of God's Word into our hearts, it protects us from deception and from sinning with our tongues. Sometimes it's hard to speak the truth. But the consequences of lying are ultimately more costly than the consequences of speaking the truth.

"*Deliver my soul, O LORD . . . from a deceitful tongue*" (Psalm 120:2 KJV). Deception can be attempting to create a better impression than is honestly true, being silent when we hear people say untruths about others, or covering up past sins. Ask God to reveal any deception in your life.

_____

_____

_____

_____

How could making yourself accountable to other believers help you be more truthful?

_____

_____

_____

_____

"*LORD, who may dwell in your sanctuary? . . . [He] who keeps his oath even when it hurts*" (Psalm 15:1, 4 NIV). Why does it displease God when we do not keep our promises or fail to fulfill a financial obligation?

_____

_____

_____

_____

Have you ever promised to pray for someone and then forgotten to do so? How can you avoid this happening in the future?

_____

_____

_____

_____

Day Four

VITAL INFORMATION

"A gossip betrays a confidence,
but a trustworthy man keeps a secret."
Proverbs 11:13 (NIV)

I chuckled as I watched an old episode of *I Love Lucy*, in which Lucy hung up from talking to Ethel on the phone, and Ricky asked Lucy, "Were you gossiping?"

Lucy answered, *"Who me? Gossiping?* I prefer to think of it as a 'mutual exchange of vital information.' Anyway, *she* was gossiping; I was just listening. That isn't gossip!"

Although we find Lucy entertaining, gossip is no laughing matter. Scripture tells us that a gossip cannot be trusted and betrays confidential information. Before repeating information, ask yourself, "Would the person who originally shared the information (or prayer request) give me permission to repeat it?"

Proverbs 17:4 says, "An evildoer listens to wicked lips, and a liar gives ear to a mischievous tongue." It's not only wrong to gossip, but it's also wrong to listen to gossip. When we do, our ears become like garbage cans.

When we spread gossip or slander about a fellow believer, we are actually sinning against our own body—for as Christians, we are all part of the body of Christ.

Second Samuel 7:28 says, "O LORD God, you are God, and your words are true." When I hear or repeat information, I want people to know that I am trustworthy—that I will speak only words that prosper others.

Why is this good advice: "If the person to whom I'm speaking isn't a part of the problem or a part of the solution, don't share it"?

 "Whoever goes about slandering reveals secrets; therefore do not associate with a simple babbler" (Proverbs 20:19). Paraphrase this verse in your own words:

 "In the same way, their [deacons'] wives are to be women worthy of respect, not malicious talkers but temperate and trustworthy in everything" (1 Timothy 3:11 NIV). According to this verse, what must be true of a woman if her husband is to be qualified for spiritual service or leadership?

 "Whoever covers an offense seeks love, but he who repeats a matter separates close friends" (Proverbs 17:9). Describe an instance when you saw this verse illustrated.

Day Five

AN INDEX OF OUR SOULS

*"The thoughts of the wicked are an abomination to
the LORD, but gracious words are pure."*
Proverbs 15:26

St. Frances de Sales said, "Our words are a faithful
index of the state of our souls." During the past two weeks
we have examined the words of our mouths and recognized a
correlation between what we say and our hearts. Today, I
want you to examine yourself—to take an index of your soul.

Below, you will find a list of several heart conditions,
along with the words that flow out of each type of heart.
Circle all of the types of heart conditions that describe you:

Foolish heart/words

• Critical heart ∼ critical words

• Mean heart ∼ mean-spirited words

• Proud heart ∼ arrogant words

• Unloving heart ∼ unkind words

• Self-centered heart ∼ self-centered words

• Angry heart ∼ angry words

• Profane heart ∼ profane words

• Impatient heart ∼ impatient words

• Discontented heart ∼ complaining words

• Deceitful heart ∼ deceitful words

Wise heart/words

• Spiritual heart ∼ spiritual words

• Kind heart ∼ kind words

• Humble heart ∼ humble words

• Loving heart ∼ loving words

• Unselfish heart ∼ other-centered wor

• Gracious heart ∼ gracious words

• Pure heart ∼ pure words

• Patient heart ∼ patient words

• Grateful heart ∼ thankful words

• Honest heart ∼ truthful words

🍇 *"Search me, O God, and know my heart"* (Psalm 139:23a). Ask the Holy Spirit to reveal the index of your soul as you prayerfully review the heart conditions you circled in today's devotion. What is God saying to you?

_____

_____

_____

_____

🍇 *"The heart of him who has understanding seeks knowledge, but the mouths of fools feed on folly"* (Proverbs 15:14). Which two or three elements of foolish heart/words do you have the greatest need to repent of?

_____

_____

_____

_____

🍇 Many of the sins of our mouths come from our proud hearts. In what areas of your life have you felt or expressed pride toward God or other people?

_____

_____

_____

_____

🍇 God sees our hearts—the foolishness and self-seeking as well as our seeking after Him. Write out a prayer of repentance—and of thanksgiving that He forgives.

_____

_____

_____

_____

Prayer

Father, Your Word is like a mirror; it shows us things we cannot see about our own hearts. As I have looked into the mirror of Your Word, I have been convicted that many times I have spoken foolishly by speaking slanderously and giving negative reports. Sometimes I have even given reports that are not true, reports that have damaged the reputations of others.

I seek Your forgiveness and ask You to change my foolish heart. Please fill my heart and mouth with words that are pure. Help me to speak good, true, kind reports with necessary words.

Cleanse me, Lord. How I need Your forgiveness and help to speak words that minister grace, health, and wholeness to others.

I pray in Jesus' name. Amen.

WORDS OF RESTRAINT

Memory Verse

"Whoever restrains his words has knowledge, and he
who has a cool spirit is a man of understanding."
Proverbs 17:27

(Record insights from this verse or ways that you apply it in
your life this week.)

_____

_____

_____

_____

Perhaps you are feeling convicted, as I have been,
through our study on the tongue. The mirror of God's Word
has exposed our hearts!

David cried out to the Lord in Psalm 26:1–3, "Vindicate
me, O LORD, for I have walked in my integrity, and I have
trusted in the LORD without wavering. Prove me, O LORD,
and try me; test my heart and my mind. For your steadfast
love is before my eyes, and I walk in your faithfulness."

The Scripture has been administering a test on our
tongues. When we hold our lives up to the Word of God,
we are all failures apart from the transforming work of God's
Spirit in our heart.

It doesn't come naturally for us to consistently speak
with wisdom and kindness. It comes supernaturally. And by
the supernatural power of the Holy Spirit, we can have wise,
kind hearts and speak wise, kind words.

Day One

A GUARDED TONGUE

"Set a guard, O LORD, over my mouth;
keep watch over the door of my lips."
Psalm 141:3

The presence of a guard indicates the possibility of danger. We don't guard something that doesn't need to be protected.

Notice where this guard is posted. Not at the ear—to protect us from being hurt by words we might hear, or at the heart—to shield us from the wounds that are sometimes caused by what others do. Rather, the Psalmist asked God to post a sentinel at his own mouth knowing that the greatest danger he faced was not what others might do to him, but rather, what he might say that would harm others.

Our tongues can be dangerous weapons. Careless, harsh, or untimely words inflict pain on those who hear. "And the tongue is a fire, a world of unrighteousness . . . setting on fire the entire course of life, and set on fire by hell" (James 3:6).

Too often we let our words run unrestrained. Even though we may later regret our words, we can never take them back. Better to set a guard at our mouth, preventing the danger from getting loose, than trying furiously to "take back" words we never should have spoken in the first place.

"Prove me, O LORD, and try me; test my heart and my mind" (Psalm 26:2). What has God been saying to you as we have been examining our words during this study?

_____

_____

_____

 "Set a guard, O LORD, over my mouth; keep watch over the door of my lips" (Psalm 141:3). Write a brief prayer expressing your desire for the Lord to control your words today.

_____

_____

_____

 "For the LORD gives wisdom; from his mouth come knowledge and understanding" (Proverbs 2:6). What role does the Word of God play in helping us speak words that are wise, kind, and gracious?

_____

_____

_____

 "Whoever keeps his mouth and his tongue keeps himself out of trouble" (Proverbs 21:23). What can you do today to guard your words?

_____

_____

_____

Day Two

HOLD THAT TONGUE

"The heart of the righteous ponders how to answer,
but the mouth of the wicked pours out evil things."
Proverbs 15:28

A New Jersey teen, Brett Banfe, decided that he was spending too much time talking and too little time listening to others. So he took a vow of silence for a year.[2]

After reading about Brett's feat, I decided to take a vow of silence myself—for just 40 hours. I didn't think it would be too hard—since I was by myself the entire time (though I'll confess I did talk to myself twice)!

That reminds me of an old story of a monk who joined a monastery where he was permitted to say only two words every ten years. After ten years, the monk said, "Bed hard!" Ten more years passed, and the monk said, "Food bad!" Finally, after ten more years, the monk spoke for the third time: "I quit!" His superior shook his head and said, "I'm not surprised. All he did for the past 30 years was complain!"

Holding our tongues is a challenge! Proverbs 29:11 (NIV) says, "A fool gives full vent to his anger, but a wise man keeps himself under control." What would an impartial observer say about your tongue? Do you say everything (or almost everything) that you think or feel? Or do you carefully choose and measure your words?

🍇 *"Do you see a man who is hasty in his words? There is more hope for a fool than for him"* (Proverbs 29:20). What are some of the sins that can result when we speak too much or too quickly? (E.g., exaggeration, gossip, insensitive comments . . .)

_____

_____

_____

_____

🍇 *"A prudent man keeps his knowledge to himself, but the heart of fools blurts out folly"* (Proverbs 12:23 NIV). What character qualities are evidenced when a person waits to speak the appropriate words at the appropriate time?

_____

_____

_____

_____

🍇 *"If one gives an answer before he hears, it is his folly and shame"* (Proverbs 18:13). Are you sometimes quick to jump to conclusions or to interrupt and respond before hearing all the facts? What does this verse say about that tendency?

_____

_____

_____

🍇 What are some practical ways you can hold your tongue today? How will these ways help communication?

_____

_____

_____

_____

Day Three

SILENCE IS GOLDEN

"When words are many, transgression is not lacking,
but whoever restrains his lips is prudent."
Proverbs 10:19

After participating in a several-hour meeting some time ago, I sensed that perhaps I had said more than I should have. I asked one of the men who was in the meeting if I had talked too much. He said, "Well, perhaps you could have condensed that long story you told!"

I am so thankful to have real friends who will help me know when I'm not walking wisely, in accordance with the Word of God. God wants our lips to be controlled by the Holy Spirit. We need His wisdom and grace to measure our words and to speak to others only after listening to Him.

People who are measured in their words are thought to be wise. Many women express frustration that their husbands don't listen to them. I don't mean to be unkind, but sometimes I wonder if men might listen more attentively if we women didn't have so much to say!

Put a checkmark by the situations below where you find it hard to hold your tongue:

❏ When tempted to criticize a pastor, ministry leader, or church service.
❏ When "interesting" information might put someone in a bad light.
❏ When a friend's experience would enhance your conversation, but you don't have permission to share her story.
❏ When you think someone made a poor—now unchangeable—choice.

 Why is it a good idea to remain silent in the above situations?

_____

_____

_____

 Fenelon says in *The Seeking Heart*, "Try to practice silence as much as general courtesy permits. Silence encourages God's presence, prevents harsh words, and causes you to be less likely to say something you will regret."[3] Why do you think it's so hard for us to hold our tongues?

_____

_____

_____

 At the end of the day, ask the Lord to bring to your mind those moments when you spoke too many words. What would have been a better response?

_____

_____

_____

Day Four

SOFT ANSWERS

"A soft answer turns away wrath,
but a harsh word stirs up anger."
Proverbs 15:1

When you turn on the television and listen to the way people speak to each other, you're likely to hear a lot of harsh, rough, angry words.

A soft or gentle answer can defuse a tense situation, but fighting words generally produce a fight! Now this doesn't mean that you should avoid speaking the truth. But, as we are reminded in Ephesians 4:15, we should speak the truth in love. Sometimes it's not so much the *words* that we say as the *spirit* in which they're said.

The men of Ephraim were easily angered and offended (see Judges 8:1–3). Yet Gideon defused their anger with a humble word. Likewise, we can create a calm climate in our homes by the way we respond to those around us, even if they are not acting as they should.

Soft, gentle words minister grace, strength, and encouragement. Try saying some of these gentle words to those around you today (beginning with those within the four walls of your home!): *I love you. . . . I'm praying for you. . . . I'm so proud of you. . . . I'm sorry I treated you that way. . . . Would you please forgive me?. . . I appreciate you. . . . You're such a blessing!*

Describe a situation when you responded to an angry person with angry words. What was the outcome? How might the outcome have been different if you had used soft words instead?

How does the atmosphere of your home change when you use soft, gentle words, instead of harsh or angry words?

"With patience a ruler may be persuaded, and a soft tongue will break a bone" (Proverbs 25:15). What does this verse say about the best way to persuade someone in authority? How might it apply to your life?

Is there anyone in your life to whom you are an authority (children, subordinates, etc.)? How do you think Proverbs 25:15 applies when you are the person in authority?

Day Five

ONE SMALL TONGUE

"Whoever keeps his mouth and
his tongue keeps himself out of trouble."
Proverbs 21:23

On September 11, 1995, a squirrel climbed onto the Metro-North Railroad power lines near New York City. This set off an electrical surge, which weakened an overhead bracket, which let a wire dangle toward the tracks, which tangled in a train, which tore down all the lines. As a result, 47,000 commuters were stuck in Manhattan for hours that evening.[4]

This story reminds me of what we've seen in our study of the tongue. Something very small can cause a lot of damage!

We might think, *It's just a tiny lie, a little argument, a few contentious words . . .* Yet we're reminded time and time again in Scripture that if we guard our mouths and tongues from saying words we'll later regret, we will save ourselves from disaster.

James 3:5 tells us that "the tongue is a small member, yet it boasts of great things. How great a forest is set ablaze by such a small fire!"

Innocent loved ones can be harmed because of our ill-spoken words. The life of a loving child, loyal spouse, or committed friend may be wounded because of just a "little" reckless word.

🍇 "*A continual dripping on a rainy day and a quarrelsome wife are alike; to restrain her is to restrain the wind or to grasp oil in one's right hand*" (Proverbs 27:15–16). In what ways might a quarrelsome woman be like a constant dripping?

_____

_____

_____

🍇 Why do you think Proverbs 27:15–16 says that restraining a quarrelsome person is like restraining the wind or grasping oil?

_____

_____

_____

_____

🍇 "*Whoever keeps his mouth and his tongue keeps himself out of trouble*" (Proverbs 21:23). Describe a time when you suffered the consequences of failing to guard your tongue.

_____

_____

_____

🍇 "*Reckless words pierce like a sword, but the tongue of the wise brings healing*" (Proverbs 12:18 NIV). How can you avoid blurting out reckless, piercing words today?

_____

_____

_____

Prayer

Father, I think of all the times I have spoken rough, harsh words . . . how often my words have failed to minister grace to the hearer.

O Lord, wash my heart; wash my mouth. Cleanse me; forgive me. Please help me speak words that are gentle, kind, sweet, and pleasant.

I do not want to be conformed to the world; I want my words to reveal the heart and the character of Jesus. I want to speak words that give life, light, hope, and strength to others.

Fill me with your Spirit, I pray. Amen.

Week Four

A HEALING TONGUE

Memory Verse

*"Gracious words are like a honeycomb,
sweetness to the soul and health to the body."*
Proverbs 16:24

(Record insights from this verse or ways that you apply it in your life this week.)

_____

_____

_____

_____

If you look up the word "healing" in a thesaurus, you will likely find these words: therapeutic, medicinal, curing. What a blessing it is to experience physical healing from sickness. An even greater blessing is when God uses us as an instrument of spiritual healing in the lives of others.

Proverbs 15:4a says, "A gentle [healing] tongue is a tree of life." Picture a lush redbud or dogwood in the peak of spring. Its branches are filled with dense blossoms announcing that spring has arrived. Its roots dig deeply into the soil, soaking up valuable nutrients, and its leaves are green and healthy—full of new life.

God says that the tongue can be like a tree of life! It can give refreshing words and encouragement to the weary. It can provide support for the anxious. It can freely give kindness to young and old alike.

May God keep watch over our lips. May our tongues minister grace, help, and healing through words of encouragement and blessing.

Day One

WISE REPROOF

"Like an earring of gold or an ornament of fine gold
is a wise man's rebuke to a listening ear."
Proverbs 25:12 (NIV)

Someone has said, "The last person to know he's got a rip in his jacket is the guy who's got it on!" I need friends who will love me enough to tell me when they see "blind spots" in my life. And I need to be willing to be that kind of friend to others.

It's so important to learn how to receive *and* how to give godly counsel and reproof. Most of us don't like the idea of being rebuked. Nor do we find it easy to rebuke others. Yet a wise person's reproof has great value and is to be desired.

According to the Scripture, a rebuke from a wise person is a *gift*. Imagine how grateful you would be if someone gave you an expensive, beautiful piece of gold jewelry—custom-designed for you! God does just that when we humbly receive wise reproof. And He does this for others when we offer wise reproof.

"Why do you see the speck in your brother's eye, but do not notice the log that is in your own eye?" (Matthew 7:3). Why is it so important to deal with our own failures and needs before pointing out the failures and needs of others?

_____

_____

_____

_____

 "Do not reprove a scoffer, or he will hate you; reprove a wise man, and he will love you" (Proverbs 9:8). What is one factor we should consider before giving a rebuke?

_____

_____

_____

_____

 "Whoever rebukes a man will afterward find more favor than he who flatters with his tongue" (Proverbs 28:23). What can help us deal with the fear of rejection?

_____

_____

_____

_____

 "Brothers, if anyone is caught in any transgression, you who are spiritual should restore him in a spirit of gentleness. Keep watch on yourself, lest you too be tempted" (Galatians 6:1). What does this verse tell us about the proper attitude for rebuking others?

_____

_____

_____

Day Two

THE GIFT OF WORDS

"To make an apt answer is a joy to a man,
and a word in season, how good it is!"
Proverbs 15:23

If you're like me, you enjoy giving and receiving gifts. Have you ever thought that each day God can work through you to give priceless gifts to your family, mate, children, roommate, fellow workers, neighbors, or friends? Wise, kind words are gifts that can change lives.

We have seen that words reflect our heart. Wise, kind words flow out of wise, kind hearts. When we fill our hearts with the Word of God, what flows from our heart to others will reflect Him. We're told in Proverbs 30:5 (KJV), "Every word of God is pure."

When our words are sifted through God's Word, they will be cherished gifts to those we love.

🍇 What would your family, friends, and colleagues say about the words of your mouth? Do they generally encourage or discourage? Do they reflect a hope in God? Explain your answer.

_____

_____

_____

_____

🍇 *"A word fitly spoken is like apples of gold in a setting of silver"* (Proverbs 25:11). Who in your life needs such words right now? How can you give them to the person (a home-made card, a phone call, even a note delivered with a vase of flowers)?

_____

_____

_____

_____

🍇 How can encouraging words be gifts that change lives?

_____

_____

_____

_____

🍇 Who can you encourage today through your words? How will you do this?

_____

_____

_____

_____

Day Three

TIME FOR A CHECK-UP

*"If you seek it like silver and search for it as for hidden
treasure, then you will understand the fear of the LORD."*
Proverbs 2:4

Have you ever lost something precious and you couldn't
rest until it was found? Perhaps you misplaced a family heir-
loom, an expensive piece of jewelry, or a cherished letter.

If you've had such an experience, you know what it's
like to look for something as though it were hidden treasure—leaving, as they say, no stone unturned.

During the past few weeks, we've traveled through the
book of Proverbs, searching for treasure that will benefit not
only ourselves, but also those around us. We've spent
almost four weeks together, and it's time for a check-up.

You will find two lists below. One illustrates
pleasant/sweet words, and the other describes some wrong
ways to use words. Put a check by the descriptions of how
you have used words during the past few days. No one will
judge your answers—this check-up is just for you.

Wrong Use of Words

❏ Gossiping
❏ Constant talking
❏ Giving false witness
❏ Rough, angry words
❏ Boasting
❏ Quarreling
❏ Insincere, flattering words
❏ Lying
❏ Slanderous words

Pleasant/Sweet Words

❏ Speaking well of the subject of gossip
❏ Patient listening
❏ Making a good report on someone
❏ Gentle, quiet words
❏ Bragging on others
❏ Mending a quarrel
❏ Sincere praise
❏ Loving truth
❏ Uplifting words

🍇 *"Search me, O God, and know my heart"* (Psalm 139:23a). Ask the Lord to search your heart and reveal the progress that you've made to bring Him glory and honor.

_____

_____

_____

🍇 Compare the consequences of saying pleasant words and using words wrongly.

_____

_____

_____

🍇 *"Whoever restrains his words has knowledge, and he who has a cool spirit is a man of understanding"* (Proverbs 17:27). Why would those who use restraint be considered knowledgeable? What does having understanding have to do with being even-tempered?

_____

_____

_____

_____

🍇 Have your words this week revealed a person of knowledge and understanding? Why or why not? What can you do today to help yourself be an even-tempered person?

_____

_____

_____

Day Four

THINK ON THESE THINGS

"Finally, brothers, whatever is true, whatever is honorable, whatever is just, whatever is pure, whatever is lovely, whatever is commendable, if there is any excellence, if there is anything worthy of praise, think about these things."
Philippians 4:8

In his wonderful book, *The Seeking Heart,* Fenelon gives this wise counsel: "What you really need to do is sit quietly before God and your active and argumentative mind would soon be calmed. God can teach you to look at each matter with a simple, clear view."[5]

When my mind gets "active and argumentative" (which actually happened within the past hour!), I'm not usually inclined to be calm and sit quietly before the Lord. Yet that's exactly what we need to do.

Philippians 4:8 tells us to think on the things that are virtuous and of good report. It's no secret that our thoughts reveal themselves in actions . . . and in words. What we think about will ultimately drive what we say and what we do. So, if we want to speak words that are true, pure, lovely, etc., we need to fill our minds with those kinds of thoughts!

Our thoughts—and our words—will be transformed as we spend time sitting (or kneeling) quietly before the Lord, letting Him teach us and showing us His view of things, as we meditate on His Word.

Be honest. Do your thoughts generally meet the standard set forth in Philippians 4:8? Explain. How could you conform your thoughts to this pattern?

_____

_____

_____

_____

 What adjustments do you need to make in light of Fenelon's advice to sit quietly before God in order to calm an "active and argumentative mind"?

_____

_____

_____

_____

 Before you go to bed tonight, jot down thoughts you had today that were:

true: _____

honest: _____

just: _____

pure: _____

lovely: _____

of good report: _____

 How would disciplining your mind each day according to Philippians 4:8 affect the way you talk to others?

_____

_____

_____

_____

Day Five

FRAGRANT WORDS

"But thanks be to God, who in Christ always leads us in triumphal procession, and through us spreads the fragrance of the knowledge of him everywhere. For we are the aroma of Christ to God among those who are being saved and among those who are perishing."
2 Corinthians 2:14-15

As we have studied various Proverbs relating to the tongue, mouth, and lips, I am more aware than ever of my need for God to keep watch over my speech. My natural self wants to blurt out words, without thinking of how they will affect others. But the Holy Spirit reminds me that my words and life can be a sweet aroma of Christ.

When we speak words that are encouraging, wise, fitting, and true, it is because of His amazing grace. It is because He has opened our eyes and hearts to the truth. I love the first stanza of John Newton's "Amazing Grace":

> *Amazing grace—how sweet the sound,*
> *That saved a wretch like me!*
> *I once was lost but now am found,*
> *Was blind but now I see.*

Although this devotional is coming to a close, our journey to glorify God with our tongues has just begun.

May you and I begin to sing and speak God's praises each day that He gives us breath, as we will spend an eternity doing in heaven! May we honor Him with our words in such a way that people marvel, "Hallelujah, what a Savior!"

How has God shown His "amazing grace" in your life?

_____

_____

_____

_____

How can the words we say be a sweet aroma of Christ to both believers and unbelievers around us? Do your words leave a "fragrance" of Jesus? Explain.

_____

_____

_____

_____

How can God's amazing grace help us speak words that are encouraging, wise, fitting, and true?

_____

_____

_____

_____

What are some specific things you will do to continue your journey to glorify God with your tongue?

_____

_____

_____

_____

Prayer

O Lord, would You do a work of grace in my heart as it relates to my tongue? I want to be a woman who opens her mouth with wisdom and who speaks with the law of kindness.

Lord, it's not just what I say—it's how I say it . . . the tone of my voice . . . the timing.

O Lord, please change me, transform me, forgive me, cleanse me, remake me, guard me. Set a guard, O Lord, over my mouth. Keep watch over the door of my lips.

May the words that come out of my mouth be words of beauty and grace that draw people to the Savior who is the living, eternal Word of God.

In Jesus' name. Amen.

NOTES

1. Rubel Shelly, Nashville, Tennessee; "Wyoming Woman Accused of Starting South Dakota Wildfire," CNN.com.
2. Cesar Soriano, "Vow of silence ends in torrent," *USA Today*, Arlingtion, VA, September 6, 2001.
3. Fenelon, *The Seeking Heart* (Jacksonville: Christian Books Publishing House, 1992), p. 71.
4. UTU News, www.utu.org, Volume 27, November 1995, Number 11.
5. Fenelon, *The Seeking Heart* (Jacksonville: Christian Books Publishing House, 1992), p. 111.

PROVERBS AND THE TONGUE

Contrasting the wise and the foolish

- The mouth of the righteous is a fountain of life, but the mouth of the wicked conceals violence. (10:11)
- The wise lay up knowledge, but the mouth of a fool brings ruin near. (10:14)
- The tongue of the righteous is choice silver; the heart of the wicked is of little worth. (10:20)
- The lips of the righteous feed many, but fools die for lack of sense. (10:21)
- The mouth of the righteous brings forth wisdom, but the perverse tongue will be cut off. (10:31)
- The lips of the righteous know what is acceptable, but the mouth of the wicked, what is perverse. (10:32)
- By the blessing of the upright a city is exalted, but by the mouth of the wicked it is overthrown. (11:11)
- By the mouth of a fool comes a rod for his back, but the lips of the wise will preserve them. (14:3)
- The tongue of the wise commends knowledge, but the mouths of fools pour out folly. (15:2)
- The heart of him who has understanding seeks knowledge, but the mouths of fools feed on folly. (15:14)
- Whoever is greedy for unjust gain troubles his own household, but he who hates bribes will live. (15:26)
- The heart of the righteous ponders how to answer, but the mouth of the wicked pours out evil things. (15:28)
- A fool's lips walk into a fight, and his mouth invites a beating. (18:6)
- A fool's mouth is his ruin, and his lips are a snare to his soul. (18:7)
- A worthless witness mocks at justice, and the mouth of the wicked devours iniquity. (19:28)

Contrasting the truthful and the deceptive

- The one who conceals hatred has lying lips, and whoever utters slander is a fool. (10:18)
- Whoever speaks the truth gives honest evidence, but a false witness utters deceit. (12:17)
- Truthful lips endure forever, but a lying tongue is but for a moment. (12:19)

- Lying lips are an abomination to the LORD, but those who act faithfully are his delight. (12:22)
- The righteous hates falsehood, but the wicked brings shame and disgrace. (13:5)
- A false witness will not go unpunished, and he who breathes out lies will not escape. (19:5)
- The getting of treasures by a lying tongue is a fleeting vapor and a snare of death. (21:6)
- Be not a witness against your neighbor without cause, and do not deceive with your lips. (24:28)
- A lying tongue hates its victims, and a flattering mouth works ruin. (26:28)
- There are six things that the LORD hates, seven that are an abomination to him: [three relate to the tongue; two relate specifically to lying] . . . a lying tongue . . . a false witness who breathes out lies, and one who sows discord among brothers. (6:16–19)

Contrasting the helpful and the hurtful
- There is one whose rash words are like sword thrusts, but the tongue of the wise brings healing. (12:18)
- Death and life are in the power of the tongue, and those who love it will eat its fruits. (18:21)
- Anxiety in a man's heart weighs him down, but a good word makes him glad. (12:25)
- Gracious words are like a honeycomb, sweetness to the soul and health to the body. (16:24)

Gossip and Slander
- Whoever goes about slandering reveals secrets, but he who is trustworthy in spirit keeps a thing covered. (11:13)
- A worthless man plots evil, and his speech is like a scorching fire. (16:27)
- A dishonest man spreads strife, and a whisperer separates close friends. (16:28)
- Whoever covers an offense seeks love, but he who repeats a matter separates close friends. (17:9)
- The words of a whisperer [gossip] are like delicious morsels [Jewish tradition: wounds]; they go down into the inner parts of the body. (18:8)

- Whoever goes about slandering reveals secrets; therefore do not associate with a simple babbler. (20:19)

How much is too much?
- When words are many, transgression is not lacking, but whoever restrains his lips is prudent. (10:19)
- A prudent man conceals knowledge, but the heart of fools proclaims folly. (12:23)
- Whoever restrains his words has knowledge, and he who has a cool spirit is a man of understanding. (17:27)
- Even a fool who keeps silent is considered wise; when he closes his lips, he is deemed intelligent. (17:28)
- If one gives an answer before he hears, it is his folly and shame. (18:13)
- A fool gives full vent to his spirit, but a wise man quietly holds it back. (29:11)
- Do you see a man who is hasty in his words? There is more hope for a fool than for him. (29:20)
- In all toil there is profit, but mere talk tends only to poverty. (14:23)

Indecency/Perversity
- The lips of the righteous know what is acceptable, but the mouth of the wicked, what is perverse. (10:32)
- The mouth of the righteous brings forth wisdom, but the perverse tongue will be cut off. (10:31)
- A man of crooked heart does not discover good, and one with a dishonest tongue falls into calamity. (17:20)
- Better is a poor person who walks in his integrity than one who is crooked in speech and is a fool. (19:1)
- A gentle [healing] tongue is a tree of life, but perverseness in it breaks the spirit. (15:4)

Boasting
- Let another praise you, and not your own mouth; a stranger, and not your own lips. (27:2)
- If you have been foolish, exalting yourself, or if you have been devising evil, put your hand on your mouth. (30:32)

Motives revealed

- The north wind brings forth rain, and a backbiting tongue, angry looks. (25:23)
- Be not envious of evil men, nor desire to be with them, for their hearts devise violence, and their lips talk of trouble. (24:1–2)
- Better to dwell in a corner of a housetop, than in a house shared with a contentious woman (21:9)
- It is better to live in a corner of the housetop than in a house shared with a quarrelsome wife. (21:19)

Persuasiveness

- A soft answer turns away wrath, but a harsh word stirs up anger. (15:1)
- The wise of heart is called discerning, and sweetness of speech increases persuasiveness. (16:21)

Correction

- Like a gold ring or an ornament of gold is a wise reprover to a listening ear. (25:12)
- Whoever rebukes a man will afterward find more favor than he who flatters with his tongue. (28:23)

Timely and Appropriate

- To make an apt answer is a joy to a man, and a word in season, how good it is! (15:23)
- A word fitly spoken is like apples of gold in a setting of silver. (25:11)

Listening

- An evildoer listens to wicked lips, and a liar gives ear to a mischievous tongue. (17:4)
- Incline your ear, and hear the words of the wise, and apply your heart to my knowledge, for it will be pleasant if you keep them within you, if all of them are ready on your lips . . . (22:17–18)

Knowledge

- Leave the presence of a fool, for there you do not meet words of knowledge. (14:7)

- There is gold and abundance of costly stones, but the lips of knowledge are a precious jewel. (20:15)

Hypocrisy
- With his mouth the godless man would destroy his neighbor, but by knowledge the righteous are delivered. (11:9)
- Like the glaze covering an earthen vessel are fervent lips with an evil heart. (26:23)
- Whoever hates disguises himself with his lips and harbors deceit in his heart; when he speaks graciously, believe him not, for there are seven abominations in his heart. (26:24–25)

Careful little mouth what you say!
- Whoever guards his mouth preserves his life; he who opens wide his lips comes to ruin. (13:3)
- Whoever keeps his mouth and his tongue keeps himself out of trouble. (21:23)
- An evil man is ensnared by the transgression of his lips, but the righteous escapes from trouble. (12:13)

Graciousness
- He who loves purity of heart, and whose speech is gracious, will have the king as his friend. (22:11)

Wisdom
- She opens her mouth with wisdom, and the teaching of kindness is on her tongue. (31:26)

Benevolence
- Open your mouth for the mute, for the rights of all who are destitute. Open your mouth, judge righteously, defend the rights of the poor and needy. (31:8–9)

Use the space below to record other Scriptures about the tongue—verses that God is using in your life:

_____
_____
_____
_____
_____
_____
_____
_____
_____
_____
_____
_____
_____
_____
_____
_____
_____
_____
_____
_____
_____
_____
_____
_____
_____
_____
_____
_____

ADDITIONAL RESOURCES

The Look: Does God Really Care What I Wear?
Booklet, 57 pages

How do you decide what to wear? And, does God have anything to do with it? Does it even matter to Him?

Has the Master Designer given us a pattern? Beyond style, what about issues of appropriateness and modesty?

Nancy Leigh DeMoss challenges Christians to ask themselves tough questions: Who decides what I wear, and why? What message does my clothing communicate? And, how can I reflect the glory of God in my wardrobe?

Biblical, practical and motivating, "The Look" challenges women (young and older), parents, and teens to discover the Truth about clothing and modestly, and to make choices based on God's eternal perspective.

Becoming a Woman of Discretion: Cultivating a Pure Heart in a Sensual World
Booklet, 40 pages

"Every wise woman builds her house; but the foolish tears it down with her hands" (Prov. 14:1).

No woman sets out to tear down her home. But it happens in many subtle ways—with our attitudes, our words, and our actions.

Walk verse-by-verse through Proverbs 7 to discover specific characteristics of the foolish woman. A series of penetrating questions is included, to help identify ways that we as women may unknowingly be "tearing down" the lives of those around us.

This message provides practical counsel to Christian women and their daughters—instruction that is greatly needed in our generation.

800-569-5959 • visit www.ReviveOurHearts.com

Lies Women Believe:
And the Truth that Sets Them Free!
Moody Publishers, 285 pages

"God can't forgive what I've done."
"I cannot walk in consistent victory over sin."
"I can't control my emotions."
"I don't have time to do everything I'm supposed to do."
"If my circumstances were different, I'd be different."

Have you ever found yourself thinking these kinds of thoughts? With courage and compassion, Nancy helps women see how they may have been deceived. She exposes forty lies commonly believed by Christian women—lies about God, sin, priorities, marriage and family, emotions, and more.

This penetrating book will help you learn how to counter and overcome Satan's deceptions with the most powerful weapon of all—God's truth!

"You will know the truth, and the truth will set you free" (John 8:32).

Buy both and SAVE!

The Companion Guide to Lies Women Believe
Moody Publishers, 128 pages

A Life-Changing Study for Groups or Individuals

This 10-week companion study to *Lies Women Believe* is ideal for a Bible study group, Sunday school class, or a small group of women.

Go deeper into God's Word, walk more fully in His grace and experience the joy of the abundant life Christ promised.

800-569-5959 • visit www.ReviveOurHearts.com

Acknowledgments

Mary Larmoyeux – Editorial Assistance
Cheryl Dunlop – Editorial Assistance
Monica Vaught – Project Coordinator
Thomas A. Jones – Design